Rejoice Always:

A 100 DAY GRATITUDE JOURNAL

WE WHO
Thirst
WOMEN

BY JESSICA JENKINS

Rejoice Always: A Gratitude Journal

© We Who Thirst | Jessica Jenkins. 2019

Published by Amazon, Print on Demand

Floral art by Opia Design Studio, www.etsy.com/shop/opiadesignsstudio.

Dear Reader,

My prayer for you is that this 100 day gratitude journal would encourage your spirit and fix your mind on Christ. I long for you to be in awe of God's character and fixated on His goodness.

The Spirit can use our practice of gratitude and rejoicing to transform our hearts and minds rooting our affections on the one we adore.

I have split each day up into four sections:

Ten Things
Quickly write down the first ten things coming to your mind that you are grateful for. This exercise gets your mind moving in the practice of thanksgiving settling into the reality of the goodness God has placed around you.

Adore God for His Character
Decide on three character traits of God to write in the blanks. Elaborate on them and how you see them evidenced in your life.

Where will I choose joy today?
Approaching our day with joy is a choice. We can choose to dwell on the negatives in our circumstances, or we can mediate on the Lord's goodness. Pick an area, or several, in which you will choose joy today. This is your act of worship!

Recent Blessings
Related to the "Ten Things," wrote down any particular blessings for which you want to thank God.

May you enjoy your Savior more richly as you feast on your remembrance of His blessings.

Jessica Jenkins has served the church as missionary, pastor's wife, women's ministry coordinator, and Bible study leader, and currently stays home with her sweet babies. She holds both a Master of Arts in Israel Studies (2008) and an Advanced Master of Divinity with a concentration in Biblical Languages (2013) . She lives in Austin, Texas, with her husband, Kevin, and her lively children (ages 4 and 2). She finds some of her greatest joy in helping women see and savor God more richly through His word. She enjoys drinking loose-leaf tea, exploring new places with her husband, and playing on the floor with her littles.

Read more of her work at wewhothirst.com.

Gratitude Practice for _____

Ten Good Things

1.
2.
3.
4.
5.
6.
7.
8.
9.
10.

Adore God for His Character

- _____
- _____
- _____

Where will I choose JOY ?

-
-
-

Recent Blessings

Gratitude Practice for _____

Ten Good Things

1.
2.
3.
4.
5.
6.
7.
8.
9.
10.

Adore God for His Character

- _____

- _____

- _____

Where will I choose JOY ?

-

-

-

Recent Blessings

Gratitude Practice for _____

Ten Good Things

1.
2.
3.
4.
5.
6.
7.
8.
9.
10.

Adore God for His Character

- _____
- _____
- _____

Where will I choose JOY ?

-
-
-

Recent Blessings

Gratitude Practice for _____

Ten Good Things

1.
2.
3.
4.
5.
6.
7.
8.
9.
10.

Adore God for His Character

- _____

- _____

- _____

Where will I choose JOY ?

-
-
-

Recent Blessings

Gratitude Practice for _____

Ten Good Things

1.
2.
3.
4.
5.
6.
7.
8.
9.
10.

Adore God for His Character

- _____

- _____

- _____

Where will I choose JOY ?

-

-

-

Recent Blessings

Gratitude Practice for _____

Ten Good Things

1.
2.
3.
4.
5.
6.
7.
8.
9.
10.

Adore God for His Character

- _____

- _____

- _____

Where will I choose JOY ?

-
-
-

Recent Blessings

Gratitude Practice for _____

Ten Good Things

1.
2.
3.
4.
5.
6.
7.
8.
9.
10.

Adore God for His Character

- _____

- _____

- _____

Where will I choose JOY ?

-
-
-

Recent Blessings

Gratitude Practice for _____

Ten Good Things

1.
2.
3.
4.
5.
6.
7.
8.
9.
10.

Adore God for His Character

- _____

- _____

- _____

Where will I choose JOY ?

-

-

-

Recent Blessings

Gratitude Practice for _____

Ten Good Things

1.
2.
3.
4.
5.
6.
7.
8.
9.
10.

Adore God for His Character

- _____
- _____
- _____

Where will I choose JOY ?

-
-
-

Recent Blessings

Gratitude Practice for _____

Ten Good Things

1.

2.

3.

4.

5.

6.

7.

8.

9.

10.

Adore God for His Character

• _____

• _____

• _____

Where will I choose JOY ?

•

•

•

Recent Blessings

Gratitude Practice for _____

Ten Good Things

1.
2.
3.
4.
5.
6.
7.
8.
9.
10.

Adore God for His Character

- _____

- _____

- _____

Where will I choose JOY ?

-

-

-

Recent Blessings

Gratitude Practice for _____

Ten Good Things

1.
2.
3.
4.
5.
6.
7.
8.
9.
10.

Adore God for His Character

- _____
- _____
- _____

Where will I choose JOY ?

-
-
-

Recent Blessings

Gratitude Practice for _____

Ten Good Things

1.
2.
3.
4.
5.
6.
7.
8.
9.
10.

Adore God for His Character

- _____

- _____

- _____

Where will I choose JOY ?

-

-

-

Recent Blessings

Gratitude Practice for _____

Ten Good Things

1.

2.

3.

4.

5.

6.

7.

8.

9.

10.

Adore God for His Character

- _____

- _____

- _____

Where will I choose JOY ?

-

-

-

Recent Blessings

Gratitude Practice for _____

Ten Good Things

1.
2.
3.
4.
5.
6.
7.
8.
9.
10.

Adore God for His Character

- _____
- _____
- _____

Where will I choose JOY ?

-
-
-

Recent Blessings

Gratitude Practice for _____

Ten Good Things

1.
2.
3.
4.
5.
6.
7.
8.
9.
10.

Adore God for His Character

• _____

• _____

• _____

Where will I choose JOY ?

•

•

•

Recent Blessings

Gratitude Practice for _____

Ten Good Things

1.
2.
3.
4.
5.
6.
7.
8.
9.
10.

Adore God for His Character

- _____
- _____
- _____

Where will I choose JOY ?

-
-
-

Recent Blessings

Gratitude Practice for _____

Ten Good Things

1.
2.
3.
4.
5.
6.
7.
8.
9.
10.

Adore God for His Character

• _____

• _____

• _____

Where will I choose JOY ?

•

•

•

Recent Blessings

Gratitude Practice for _____

Ten Good Things

1.
2.
3.
4.
5.
6.
7.
8.
9.
10.

Adore God for His Character

- _____
- _____
- _____

Where will I choose JOY ?

-
-
-

Recent Blessings

Gratitude Practice for _____

Ten Good Things

1.
2.
3.
4.
5.
6.
7.
8.
9.
10.

Adore God for His Character

- _____

- _____

- _____

Where will I choose JOY ?

-

-

-

Recent Blessings

Gratitude Practice for _____

Ten Good Things

1.
2.
3.
4.
5.
6.
7.
8.
9.
10.

Adore God for His Character

- _____

- _____

- _____

Where will I choose JOY ?

-

-

-

Recent Blessings

Gratitude Practice for _____

Ten Good Things

1.
2.
3.
4.
5.
6.
7.
8.
9.
10.

Adore God for His Character

- _____

- _____

- _____

Where will I choose JOY ?

-

-

-

Recent Blessings

Gratitude Practice for _____

Ten Good Things

1.
2.
3.
4.
5.
6.
7.
8.
9.
10.

Adore God for His Character

- _____
- _____
- _____

Where will I choose JOY ?

-
-
-

Recent Blessings

Gratitude Practice for _____

Ten Good Things

1.

2.

3.

4.

5.

6.

7.

8.

9.

10.

Adore God for His Character

- _____

- _____

- _____

Where will I choose JOY ?

-

-

-

Recent Blessings

Gratitude Practice for _____

Ten Good Things

1.
2.
3.
4.
5.
6.
7.
8.
9.
10.

Adore God for His Character

• _____

• _____

• _____

Where will I choose JOY ?

•

•

•

Recent Blessings

Gratitude Practice for _____

Ten Good Things

1.

2.

3.

4.

5.

6.

7.

8.

9.

10.

Adore God for His Character

- _____

- _____

- _____

Where will I choose JOY ?

-

-

-

Recent Blessings

Gratitude Practice for _____

Ten Good Things

1.
2.
3.
4.
5.
6.
7.
8.
9.
10.

Adore God for His Character

• _____

• _____

• _____

Where will I choose JOY ?

•

•

•

Recent Blessings

Gratitude Practice for _____

Ten Good Things

1.
2.
3.
4.
5.
6.
7.
8.
9.
10.

Adore God for His Character

- _____

- _____

- _____

Where will I choose JOY ?

-

-

-

Recent Blessings

Gratitude Practice for _____

Ten Good Things

1.
2.
3.
4.
5.
6.
7.
8.
9.
10.

Adore God for His Character

- _____
- _____
- _____

Where will I choose JOY ?

-
-
-

Recent Blessings

Gratitude Practice for _____

Ten Good Things

1.

2.

3.

4.

5.

6.

7.

8.

9.

10.

Adore God for His Character

- _____

- _____

- _____

Where will I choose JOY ?

-

-

-

Recent Blessings

Gratitude Practice for _____

Ten Good Things

1.
2.
3.
4.
5.
6.
7.
8.
9.
10.

Adore God for His Character

• _____

• _____

• _____

Where will I choose JOY ?

•

•

•

Recent Blessings

Gratitude Practice for _____

Ten Good Things

1.
2.
3.
4.
5.
6.
7.
8.
9.
10.

Adore God for His Character

- _____

- _____

- _____

Where will I choose JOY ?

-
-
-

Recent Blessings

Gratitude Practice for _____

Ten Good Things

1.
2.
3.
4.
5.
6.
7.
8.
9.
10.

Adore God for His Character

- _____
- _____
- _____

Where will I choose JOY ?

-
-
-

Recent Blessings

Gratitude Practice for _____

Ten Good Things

1.

2.

3.

4.

5.

6.

7.

8.

9.

10.

Adore God for His Character

- _____

- _____

- _____

Where will I choose JOY ?

-

-

-

Recent Blessings

Gratitude Practice for _____

Ten Good Things

1.
2.
3.
4.
5.
6.
7.
8.
9.
10.

Adore God for His Character

• _____

• _____

• _____

Where will I choose JOY ?

•

•

•

Recent Blessings

Gratitude Practice for _____

Ten Good Things

1.
2.
3.
4.
5.
6.
7.
8.
9.
10.

Adore God for His Character

- _____
- _____
- _____

Where will I choose JOY ?

-
-
-

Recent Blessings

Gratitude Practice for _____

Ten Good Things

1.
2.
3.
4.
5.
6.
7.
8.
9.
10.

Adore God for His Character

- _____
- _____
- _____

Where will I choose JOY ?

-
-
-

Recent Blessings

Gratitude Practice for _____

Ten Good Things

1.
2.
3.
4.
5.
6.
7.
8.
9.
10.

Adore God for His Character

- _____

- _____

- _____

Where will I choose JOY ?

-
-
-

Recent Blessings

Gratitude Practice for _____

Ten Good Things

1.
2.
3.
4.
5.
6.
7.
8.
9.
10.

Adore God for His Character

- _____

- _____

- _____

Where will I choose JOY ?

-

-

-

Recent Blessings

Gratitude Practice for _____

Ten Good Things

1.
2.
3.
4.
5.
6.
7.
8.
9.
10.

Adore God for His Character

- _____
- _____
- _____

Where will I choose JOY ?

-
-
-

Recent Blessings

Gratitude Practice for _____

Ten Good Things

1.
2.
3.
4.
5.
6.
7.
8.
9.
10.

Adore God for His Character

- _____
- _____
- _____

Where will I choose JOY ?

-
-
-

Recent Blessings

Gratitude Practice for _____

Ten Good Things

1.

2.

3.

4.

5.

6.

7.

8.

9.

10.

Adore God for His Character

- _____

- _____

- _____

Where will I choose JOY ?

-

-

-

Recent Blessings

Gratitude Practice for _____

Ten Good Things

1.
2.
3.
4.
5.
6.
7.
8.
9.
10.

Adore God for His Character

- _____
- _____
- _____

Where will I choose JOY ?

-
-
-

Recent Blessings

Gratitude Practice for _____

Ten Good Things

1.

2.

3.

4.

5.

6.

7.

8.

9.

10.

Adore God for His Character

- _____

- _____

- _____

Where will I choose JOY ?

-

-

-

Recent Blessings

Gratitude Practice for _____

Ten Good Things

1.
2.
3.
4.
5.
6.
7.
8.
9.
10.

Adore God for His Character

- _____

- _____

- _____

Where will I choose JOY ?

-
-
-

Recent Blessings

Gratitude Practice for _____

Ten Good Things

1.
2.
3.
4.
5.
6.
7.
8.
9.
10.

Adore God for His Character

- _____
- _____
- _____

Where will I choose JOY ?

-
-
-

Recent Blessings

Gratitude Practice for _____

Ten Good Things

1.
2.
3.
4.
5.
6.
7.
8.
9.
10.

Adore God for His Character

- _____

- _____

- _____

Where will I choose JOY ?

-

-

-

Recent Blessings

Gratitude Practice for _____

Ten Good Things

1.
2.
3.
4.
5.
6.
7.
8.
9.
10.

Adore God for His Character

• _____

• _____

• _____

Where will I choose JOY ?

•

•

•

Recent Blessings

Gratitude Practice for _____

Ten Good Things

1.
2.
3.
4.
5.
6.
7.
8.
9.
10.

Adore God for His Character

• _____

• _____

• _____

Where will I choose JOY ?

•

•

•

Recent Blessings

Gratitude Practice for _____

Ten Good Things

1.
2.
3.
4.
5.
6.
7.
8.
9.
10.

Adore God for His Character

* _____

* _____

* _____

Where will I choose JOY ?

*

*

*

Recent Blessings

Gratitude Practice for _____

Ten Good Things

1.
2.
3.
4.
5.
6.
7.
8.
9.
10.

Adore God for His Character

- _____

- _____

- _____

Where will I choose JOY ?

-
-
-

Recent Blessings

Gratitude Practice for _____

Ten Good Things

1.
2.
3.
4.
5.
6.
7.
8.
9.
10.

Adore God for His Character

- _____

- _____

- _____

Where will I choose JOY ?

-

-

-

Recent Blessings

Gratitude Practice for _____

Ten Good Things

1.
2.
3.
4.
5.
6.
7.
8.
9.
10.

Adore God for His Character

- _____

- _____

- _____

Where will I choose JOY ?

-
-
-

Recent Blessings

Gratitude Practice for _____

Ten Good Things

1.
2.
3.
4.
5.
6.
7.
8.
9.
10.

Adore God for His Character

- _____

- _____

- _____

Where will I choose JOY ?

-

-

-

Recent Blessings

Gratitude Practice for _____

Ten Good Things

1.

2.

3.

4.

5.

6.

7.

8.

9.

10.

Adore God for His Character

- _____

- _____

- _____

Where will I choose JOY ?

-

-

-

Recent Blessings

Gratitude Practice for _____

Ten Good Things

1.
2.
3.
4.
5.
6.
7.
8.
9.
10.

Adore God for His Character

- _____

- _____

- _____

Where will I choose JOY ?

-

-

-

Recent Blessings

Gratitude Practice for _____

Ten Good Things

1.
2.
3.
4.
5.
6.
7.
8.
9.
10.

Adore God for His Character

- _____
- _____
- _____

Where will I choose JOY ?

-
-
-

Recent Blessings

Gratitude Practice for _____

Ten Good Things

1.
2.
3.
4.
5.
6.
7.
8.
9.
10.

Adore God for His Character

- _____

- _____

- _____

Where will I choose JOY ?

-

-

-

Recent Blessings

Gratitude Practice for _____

Ten Good Things

1.
2.
3.
4.
5.
6.
7.
8.
9.
10.

Adore God for His Character

- _____
- _____
- _____

Where will I choose JOY ?

-
-
-

Recent Blessings

Gratitude Practice for _____

Ten Good Things

1.
2.
3.
4.
5.
6.
7.
8.
9.
10.

Adore God for His Character

- _____

- _____

- _____

Where will I choose JOY ?

-

-

-

Recent Blessings

Gratitude Practice for _____

Ten Good Things

1.

2.

3.

4.

5.

6.

7.

8.

9.

10.

Adore God for His Character

• _____

• _____

• _____

Where will I choose JOY ?

•

•

•

Recent Blessings

Gratitude Practice for _____

Ten Good Things

1.
2.
3.
4.
5.
6.
7.
8.
9.
10.

Adore God for His Character

• _____

• _____

• _____

Where will I choose JOY ?

•

•

•

Recent Blessings

Gratitude Practice for _____

Ten Good Things

1.

2.

3.

4.

5.

6.

7.

8.

9.

10.

Adore God for His Character

• _____

• _____

• _____

Where will I choose JOY ?

•

•

•

Recent Blessings

Gratitude Practice for _____

Ten Good Things

1.
2.
3.
4.
5.
6.
7.
8.
9.
10.

Adore God for His Character

- _____

- _____

- _____

Where will I choose JOY ?

-

-

-

Recent Blessings

Gratitude Practice for _____

Ten Good Things

1.
2.
3.
4.
5.
6.
7.
8.
9.
10.

Adore God for His Character

- _____
- _____
- _____

Where will I choose JOY ?

-
-
-

Recent Blessings

Gratitude Practice for _____

Ten Good Things

1.
2.
3.
4.
5.
6.
7.
8.
9.
10.

Adore God for His Character

- _____

- _____

- _____

Where will I choose JOY ?

-

-

-

Recent Blessings

Gratitude Practice for _____

Ten Good Things

1.
2.
3.
4.
5.
6.
7.
8.
9.
10.

Adore God for His Character

- _____
- _____
- _____

Where will I choose JOY ?

-
-
-

Recent Blessings

Gratitude Practice for _____

Ten Good Things

1.
2.
3.
4.
5.
6.
7.
8.
9.
10.

Adore God for His Character

- _____

- _____

- _____

Where will I choose JOY ?

-

-

-

Recent Blessings

Gratitude Practice for _____

Ten Good Things

1.
2.
3.
4.
5.
6.
7.
8.
9.
10.

Adore God for His Character

- _____

- _____

- _____

Where will I choose JOY ?

-

-

-

Recent Blessings

Gratitude Practice for _____

Ten Good Things

1.
2.
3.
4.
5.
6.
7.
8.
9.
10.

Adore God for His Character

- _____

- _____

- _____

Where will I choose JOY ?

-

-

-

Recent Blessings

Gratitude Practice for _____

Ten Good Things

1.
2.
3.
4.
5.
6.
7.
8.
9.
10.

Adore God for His Character

• _____

• _____

• _____

Where will I choose JOY ?

•

•

•

Recent Blessings

Gratitude Practice for _____

Ten Good Things

1.
2.
3.
4.
5.
6.
7.
8.
9.
10.

Adore God for His Character

- _____

- _____

- _____

Where will I choose JOY ?

-

-

-

Recent Blessings

Gratitude Practice for _____

Ten Good Things

1.
2.
3.
4.
5.
6.
7.
8.
9.
10.

Adore God for His Character

- _____
- _____
- _____

Where will I choose JOY ?

-
-
-

Recent Blessings

Gratitude Practice for _____

Ten Good Things

1.
2.
3.
4.
5.
6.
7.
8.
9.
10.

Adore God for His Character

- _____

- _____

- _____

Where will I choose JOY ?

-

-

-

Recent Blessings

Gratitude Practice for _____

Ten Good Things

1.

2.

3.

4.

5.

6.

7.

8.

9.

10.

Adore God for His Character

- _____

- _____

- _____

Where will I choose JOY ?

-

-

-

Recent Blessings

Gratitude Practice for _____

Ten Good Things

1.
2.
3.
4.
5.
6.
7.
8.
9.
10.

Adore God for His Character

- _____

- _____

- _____

Where will I choose JOY ?

-

-

-

Recent Blessings

Gratitude Practice for _____

Ten Good Things

1.
2.
3.
4.
5.
6.
7.
8.
9.
10.

Adore God for His Character

- _____

- _____

- _____

Where will I choose JOY ?

-

-

-

Recent Blessings

Gratitude Practice for _____

Ten Good Things

1.
2.
3.
4.
5.
6.
7.
8.
9.
10.

Adore God for His Character

- _____

- _____

- _____

Where will I choose JOY ?

-

-

-

Recent Blessings

Gratitude Practice for _____

Ten Good Things

1.
2.
3.
4.
5.
6.
7.
8.
9.
10.

Adore God for His Character

- _____
- _____
- _____

Where will I choose JOY ?

-
-
-

Recent Blessings

Gratitude Practice for _____

Ten Good Things

1.
2.
3.
4.
5.
6.
7.
8.
9.
10.

Adore God for His Character

• _____

• _____

• _____

Where will I choose JOY ?

•

•

•

Recent Blessings

Gratitude Practice for _____

Ten Good Things

1.
2.
3.
4.
5.
6.
7.
8.
9.
10.

Adore God for His Character

• _____

• _____

• _____

Where will I choose JOY ?

•

•

•

Recent Blessings

Gratitude Practice for _____

Ten Good Things

1.
2.
3.
4.
5.
6.
7.
8.
9.
10.

Adore God for His Character

- _____

- _____

- _____

Where will I choose JOY ?

-

-

-

Recent Blessings

Gratitude Practice for _____

Ten Good Things

1.
2.
3.
4.
5.
6.
7.
8.
9.
10.

Adore God for His Character

- _____

- _____

- _____

Where will I choose JOY ?

-

-

-

Recent Blessings

Gratitude Practice for _____

Ten Good Things

1.
2.
3.
4.
5.
6.
7.
8.
9.
10.

Adore God for His Character

- _____

- _____

- _____

Where will I choose JOY ?

-

-

-

Recent Blessings

Gratitude Practice for _____

Ten Good Things

1.
2.
3.
4.
5.
6.
7.
8.
9.
10.

Adore God for His Character

- _____
- _____
- _____

Where will I choose JOY ?

-
-
-

Recent Blessings

Gratitude Practice for _____

Ten Good Things

1.
2.
3.
4.
5.
6.
7.
8.
9.
10.

Adore God for His Character

- _____

- _____

- _____

Where will I choose JOY ?

-

-

-

Recent Blessings

Gratitude Practice for _____

Ten Good Things

1.
2.
3.
4.
5.
6.
7.
8.
9.
10.

Adore God for His Character

- _____
- _____
- _____

Where will I choose JOY ?

-
-
-

Recent Blessings

Gratitude Practice for _____

Ten Good Things

1.
2.
3.
4.
5.
6.
7.
8.
9.
10.

Adore God for His Character

- _____

- _____

- _____

Where will I choose JOY ?

-

-

-

Recent Blessings

Gratitude Practice for _____

Ten Good Things

1.
2.
3.
4.
5.
6.
7.
8.
9.
10.

Adore God for His Character

- _____
- _____
- _____

Where will I choose JOY ?

-
-
-

Recent Blessings

Gratitude Practice for _____

Ten Good Things

1.
2.
3.
4.
5.
6.
7.
8.
9.
10.

Adore God for His Character

- _____

- _____

- _____

Where will I choose JOY ?

-

-

-

Recent Blessings

Gratitude Practice for _____

Ten Good Things

1.

2.

3.

4.

5.

6.

7.

8.

9.

10.

Adore God for His Character

- _____

- _____

- _____

Where will I choose JOY ?

-

-

-

Recent Blessings

Gratitude Practice for _____

Ten Good Things

1.
2.
3.
4.
5.
6.
7.
8.
9.
10.

Adore God for His Character

* _____

* _____

* _____

Where will I choose JOY ?

*

*

*

Recent Blessings

Gratitude Practice for _____

Ten Good Things

1.
2.
3.
4.
5.
6.
7.
8.
9.
10.

Adore God for His Character

- _____
- _____
- _____

Where will I choose JOY ?

-
-
-

Recent Blessings

Gratitude Practice for _____

Ten Good Things

1.
2.
3.
4.
5.
6.
7.
8.
9.
10.

Adore God for His Character

- _____

- _____

- _____

Where will I choose JOY ?

-

-

-

Recent Blessings

Gratitude Practice for _____

Ten Good Things

1.
2.
3.
4.
5.
6.
7.
8.
9.
10.

Adore God for His Character

- _____

- _____

- _____

Where will I choose JOY ?

-

-

-

Recent Blessings

Gratitude Practice for _____

Ten Good Things

1.
2.
3.
4.
5.
6.
7.
8.
9.
10.

Adore God for His Character

- _____

- _____

- _____

Where will I choose JOY ?

-

-

-

Recent Blessings

Gratitude Practice for _____

Ten Good Things

1.
2.
3.
4.
5.
6.
7.
8.
9.
10.

Adore God for His Character

- _____

- _____

- _____

Where will I choose JOY ?

-

-

-

Recent Blessings

Gratitude Practice for _____

Ten Good Things

1.
2.
3.
4.
5.
6.
7.
8.
9.
10.

Adore God for His Character

- _____

- _____

- _____

Where will I choose JOY ?

-

-

-

Recent Blessings

Gratitude Practice for _____

Ten Good Things

1.
2.
3.
4.
5.
6.
7.
8.
9.
10.

Adore God for His Character

- _____
- _____
- _____

Where will I choose JOY ?

-
-
-

Recent Blessings

Gratitude Practice for _____

Ten Good Things

1.
2.
3.
4.
5.
6.
7.
8.
9.
10.

Adore God for His Character

- _____

- _____

- _____

Where will I choose JOY ?

-
-
-

Recent Blessings

Made in the USA
Coppell, TX
07 December 2022

88060268R00060